Rain
Shadow

Rain
Shadow

Nicholas
Bradley

 THE UNIVERSITY
of ALBERTA PRESS

Published by

The University of Alberta Press
Ring House 2
Edmonton, Alberta, Canada T6G 2E1
www.uap.ualberta.ca

Library and Archives Canada Cataloguing in Publication

Bradley, Nicholas, 1978–, author
Rain shadow / Nicholas Bradley.

(Robert Kroetsch series)
Poems.
Issued in print and electronic formats.
ISBN 978–1–77212–370–8 (softcover).—
ISBN 978–1–77212–389–0 (PDF)

I. Title. II. Series: Robert Kroetsch series

PS8603.R33175R35 2018   C811'.6   C2017-907093-2
C2017-907094-0

First edition, first printing, 2018.
First printed and bound in Canada by Houghton Boston Printers, Saskatoon, Saskatchewan.
Editing and proofreading by Alice Major.

A volume in the Robert Kroetsch Series.

The University of Alberta Press is committed to protecting our natural environment.
As part of our efforts, this book is printed on Enviro Paper: it contains 100% post-consumer
recycled fibres and is acid- and chlorine-free.

The University of Alberta Press gratefully acknowledges the support received for its publishing
program from the Government of Canada, the Canada Council for the Arts,
and the Government of Alberta through the Alberta Media Fund.

"Avalanche Bulletin": Quoted passage © 2003. Text reprinted with permission
of the publisher from *The ABCs of Avalanche Safety* by Sue A. Ferguson and
Edward R. LaChapelle, Mountaineers Books, Seattle.

"Guillemots et guillemets": The passage from *The Elements of Typographic Style* appears
with the permission of the author and Hartley & Marks Publishers.

"Maundy Thursday": Lines from "Nicholas Ferrer," by Ted Hughes, are reproduced
with the permission of Faber and Faber Ltd.

For Erin, sea-discoverer

Ante mare et terras et quod tegit omnia caelum
unus erat toto naturae vultus in orbe
quem dixere chaos
　　　　—*Ovid,* Metamorphoses

Before the Seas, and this Terrestrial Ball,
And Heav'ns high Canopy, that covers all,
One was the Face of Nature; if a Face,
Rather a rude and indigested Mass:
A lifeless Lump, unfashion'd, and unfram'd;
Of jarring Seeds; and justly Chaos nam'd.
　　　　—*translated by John Dryden*

Contents

II | Thisness

III | Instructions for Travel

IV | Metamorphoses

I

The Same
Mountain Twice

The Same Mountain Twice

What next? When I was half the age
I am now, I watched a man pick black-
berries in brambles across the road. Juice
and blood gloved his hands. I would have
said then that the violence and dread
of a time of war purpled his fingers. Or was
it the wealth of a ripe era? Now I revise:
the man, the street, the blackberries
were simply there on Ash Road. I was half my age.

When we took in the Chittenden Locks last
month, we strolled along the edge of Shilshole Bay,
eyeballing boats—we'd buy that one someday,
or this one, and be fishers, who are free, or make
a killing in razor clams and Dungeness crabs.
Omens were everywhere, like barnacles
on dry-docked hulls. Salt chuck slapped
wooden vessels, the concrete breakwater.
Limpets and mussels glistened in shallows.
We caught the last light on the Olympics
across Puget Sound. Lurid oysters delighted
in the salty stink while we read stern
names, briny and knotted, on the monument
to the sons of Leif Erikson—Olaf, Dag, Arne,
Einar. *Coho, sockeye, chinook, kokanee,*
chum. Did the magic words bring these Vikings
luck? The odds favoured disaster. Boats
on fire, brothers lost at sea. *Skagit, Tacoma,*
Duwamish: pacific places whisper, beckon.
When the half-moon came out we finished
with Norwegian inscriptions and foraged for dinner
on Ballard's Beemer-fringed streets.

In the morning I watched Mount Rainier
till clouds rolled in. Then clear skies that evening
divulged the volcano again—immense,
aloof, a portent in andesite. I thought
of blackberries and the crack of gunshot
when a slab releases to loose an avalanche.
The proximate realm so far from our own
explodes this sphere, remakes it. All the world's
wonders are on display when gates and valves
haul keels up the Ship Canal while salmon
climb the fish ladder. A duet: *alto*
and *basso*. Everything, Heraclitus said,
is arsy-versy for a time. The ocean
is shipwrecked, and black bear cubs
refuse to descend from trees. I'm neither
mountain nor monument. Your heart
traps mine as summits catch storms. Call
this calm the rain shadow. What will
remain? Zero moves through all things.

~ Seattle

Ostrea lurida: *the Olympia oyster*

Gray Wolf Pass

No wolves—only a signpost circled by slabs,
ridge after edge, and a tangerine hint below
cobalt as day subsides into lignite. Height's
a salve. Home is not the only home we have.

Glacial Suite

after Richard Dauenhauer

A crevasse is a cradle
of nothing. It collects
slender air and rocks
it into deep, slanted
silence. Nothing, woken,
crawls over the lip
to the icefield. The fissure
takes nothing in, breathes
nothing out. The chill,
startling bite on no one's
lips, in nobody's lungs,
is the glacier in flight.

At the beginning of the world,
at the sphere's edge,
is an abyss.
In that chasm is the world's salvation.
Nothing is suspended, weightless.

Fear of the corner
between this and that
is reasonable: the cleft
will kill. Distress
is warming. Ice burns
and waves of light
break on the breach's shore.

A body in the crevasse melts
the ice. Night refreezes
the weakness. The form is entombed
in the crystalline hiatus
and will be until it ceases
to be and becomes not ice
but part of the ice,
the ingrained cold that is
not permanent at all.

Coming down
the Coleman,
cutting across the gradient,
sidestepping through
saturated snow,
I walk with the parallel
beneath me saluting.

Dark against the névé
and the white sky, the split
hails the air,
coaxes light to it
and has to be held
by travellers
at a distance.
In one hand
the piolet.
Nothing in the other.

The convexity of the sky
is a cradle overturned,
its rocking so modest
it could be taken for calm.

My darkest heart is a fractured
landscape. The route across
threads back and forth, skirting
cracks, crossing snow
bridges, leading nowhere.

Your starless heart
is a splintered glacier
with nothing running
through channels' embracing
arms. Tributaries overrun.

My heart and yours, crow, are one.

Ice in the hand becomes water
and, alive, is life.

A mouth of cold air speaks truly
and a mouth of ice clearly—
with brittle beauty.

A mouth of snow stops speech
to let cold seep in,
where it would stay.

The bright blue of the crevasse
in strong sun
is the bluest blue.
The white of the snow
is the whitest white
at least for a time,
at least for now,

that dwindling
moment.

The time turned to strata
in ancient miles of ice
is waiting. The lingering
cold is patience
exhaling. In the bed
of the crevasse all
is in repose. The crevasse
cradles nothing.

~ **Mount Baker**

Appleton Pass
Watershed Nocturne

The darkening darkness on the Pacific offing,
the convening blackness over the foreland,
the spreading pall across the mind's eye,
and the mind
pause at dusk
as if the wind had shifted
and for an instant the tern were netted
as its feathers captured the encroaching current.
Then darkness and mind resume. The absence of light
unrolls, satellite peaks set aswim by night.

Song of the Notch

Now is the time that face should form another
—Shakespeare, Sonnet 3

In the Queets Basin there is no nature
but the nature of things. No time but time
of loam, the clock that peals from moment
to moment to end, from age to epoch
to end. On the scrabbly ridge that divides
one valley from the other—a gravel
circus, a festival of chipped teeth—hands
pass six and twelve. There is no middle
but the middle of things, no midpoint, no
path. What rises in the morning? No sun.
At night? No moon. As headwalls watch, no egg
hatches in another bird's heather nest
except the oval naught (a moulin, a mirror)
through which door springs elfin hoarfrost singing
Cuckoo, cuckoo, the faces are forming.

~ **Dodwell-Rixon Pass**

Song of the Wind-Loaded Ledges

Snacking divinities snap frangible
ridges off the milky walls
of Bourgeau's range. *Letters of ice*
drop into the valley. Warmth
and hawks rise in reply. Can you
see the haze beyond the treed
slope's long curve? *The forest's*
fuse has been lit. Miles
away, the overwintering dipper
praises glacial silt. *A mallard*
answers. Darkness and light nest
in airy mountain caves. *I feel your hand*
in the wind. A seam of air cuts
through the massif. *I hear your voice*
in ruptures, in high seas of snow.

~ Banff; Mount Deception

Larches on the Continental Divide

Inhales the alp,
inhales the wind.

Exhales the scarp,
exhales the cirriform smear.

Inhales the ultramontane coulee,
inhales the meandering mind.

Exhales the couloir,
exhales the enlivened eye

and comes the larches' change.
Our lungs, nightfall, cinders,

and the bowl of the burnt valley
are cupped by mountains' unlit angles.

On the basin's floor and curving walls
turn sudden tides of invisible trees

of the genus *Blackness*,
the species *blackness*.

Cadmium yellow
sparks combustible tarns.

~ **Off Highway 93**

Whiteout in May

Pursued by the wolf of winter I fall,
learning quickly to be slow. Bushy clouds
cover two thirds of the soundless hill

before my nonplussed eyes. Now its glaucous
base shades into chalk. Snow—though forecasts
predicted rain and rising temperatures

to spring avalanches. Tonight I'll wander
up the trail another time to see vapour
from inside. As wet stars and dendrites

splatter the roads, I think that memories
of the Ice Age must lurk in the mind's
fallow. No—I can hardly remember

last week. I picture lodgepoles and the western
redcedars that survive millennia.
This winter, they say, was one for the books,

and summer will be a scorcher.
As blizzard sees scarp, as ridge glares at wolf,
so the cirque spies the cub. Tonight I'll try

to know winter from within—to feel sap
and sleep suspended in air. Let's take
an error's measure. Come. We must be snow.

~ Banff

Some Goats

The barrelling fog clears.
On the attenuated ledge
above the hanging valley,
five sudden goats. Air settles
lightly on crumbling stone.
They pick their way
across the crag without
stumbling or slipping,
taking no notice of heights
as they search for the least
sterile of rocks and transmute
nothing into lunch. At three thousand
metres, hobnailed conundrums
munch. Some goats are puzzles.
Some goats are postcards
mailed by mountains to say
Wish you were here.

Fat Salmon in the Clearwater River

Look left: squint
to see coho flung
to sun from blue.
That one jumped
too soon: turbulent
waters swirl
upstream still.
It won't hurdle
the rapids. Too fast.
Too steep. This deep,
calm pool is its last
locale. Slamming
against cantilevered
rocks, the salmon thrusts
but fails to thirl
cobbled barriers.

Read the polished,
striated stone,
its thrill and lift
time's index.
Remember that
canny, submarine
gods must have sanctioned
the spectacle, deemed
it necessary
and good.

Sea to Sky

Highway 99 south of Whistler
is lousy with wet bears
who think the rainforest
on one side is different
from the trees on the other.
Cars litter the road's
edge. Protruding
from windows, telephoto
snouts snuffle waterlogged air.
Digital single-lens reflex
cameras rev in drive mode,
framing the tableau
eight times a second.
Shutters jackhammer
open and shut. Semis
blow by, monsooning
the mob. Binary cubs
hibernate on memory
cards till the first blush
of download. Drivers
resume speed, zooming
to town at 90 per. Gondolas
ferry them to new vistas
high above the wilderness
that data roam. Left
behind, listless furballs,
bored by scenery, saunter
toward forsaken campsites
to give garbage cans
a desultory mauling. In old
paintings, beneficent sheep
nuzzle picnicking shepherds.
Here not even clouds are woolly.

Port Angeles

Jobs Not Parks bark signs
along the highway
that carries us
through Douglas-fir
plantations to the seaboard.
It is impossible to argue
or choose on the wet,
winding 101,
which relinquishes
us as it led us
away. *Next Harvest:*
50 Years. We promise
to return. Logging
corporations will outlive us,
the cut block outlast us,
and maybe the gas
station in sodden Forks
that fuels us out and back.
While we wait
at this finistère
for the ferry, foretokens
wash with grey scum
onto the beach to yield
us time and place. Drizzle
falls delicately on Ediz
Hook as we hesitate
before exchanging
one shore for another.

Quadrilateral

When the shivery whiff schemes with evening's
·angle to uncloak two volcanos
and the cumulus-piercing point
of a clastic wedge—Baker to the east,
Olympus to the south, Rainier,
the diametric corner—you could catch,
from the observation deck on this low
hill, a sense of order, of what the mind
seeks and the heart minds. Surprise, direction.
Poise or precision. X to mark the spot.
But gloveless fingers ache. Muddy shoes
are ruined. The selfish body wants
to leave. No one can stand mountains for long.
The car's impatient, home insistent.

                           Quit
the concrete bucket, cross the hormonal
lot full of high schoolers hotboxing
borrowed SUVs, forget isolines
and elevations.

              Illuminated
in terminal minutes, the rectangle
floats—a hammered sheet, an Alpine nimbus.
Prominences await the right second
to erupt.

                                     ~ Victoria

Fall Classic

Charring the skin of rocks
on the foreshore, harrowing
the beach grass (*Ammophila
arenaria*: invasive weed,
evocative nuisance), dusting
bleached blades with salt,
brisk winds drop hints
of winter on the scape.

Ducking its head over
and over in the bay,
a gull, in a mania
of cleanliness—who knows?
—or supracharacteristic
hydrophilia, ushers me
to what lingers, as summer
expires, under the soapy

surface: ordinary
refuse, vegetation, old tires.
Muck and timber. I retrieve
my breath beneath waving
cypresses (*C. macrocarpa*)
as the breeze stiffens. Each
branch fans October
with infinite forbearance.

Come on—that's wishful
thinking. Oakland hosts
the Tigers tonight. Every TV
in the hotel is primed. The American
League Division Series (2–2) is up
for grabs and someone's season's over.

BART trains hum to the Coliseum.
Cypresses hope against hazard

that Justin Verlander has
an off night, is shellacked
by Detroit's big bats. Stop. That's
wrong, too. But the plain,
incontrovertible truth—that mere
branches of mere evergreens
sway according to mere
(although changing) atmospheric

pressure—is as dull, piffling,
and brutal as Verlander's line alone
will be: eight innings, two hits, one
walk, ten Ks, the win for Motor City.
Bye-bye, A's. See you in Spring
Training. It will also matter,
for a time, whether every four-seamer
is fast enough to keep Coco Crisp

(#4) from grasping what's coming.
Possibility counts. Dusty rolling
hills don't contradict me, nor
do rocks bristle. I ran six
and a half miles to end where I started.
In three quarters of an hour
the gull has buggered off,
the zephyr shifted, sped up.

Fog-loving cypresses,
unruffled, slightly toxic, keep quiet
and their worries to themselves.
The branches are windswept.
No elongated limbs hover
or caper like spinnakers and lunge

for contact with the element.
The trick's to untrain eyes

and mind to perceive the swishing
tree and not think *wind*
but *exultation*, which is about
as easy as spotting the heater
as it leaves the pitcher's
whipping hand. Just ask Coco.
The world is present
but not the whole world.

North of Alameda, Contra Costa
County takes the field—the opposite shore.
Coast and its complement
coexist for the moment. The hyper gull
in San Francisco's salt mere
meant no plangency. I part
the Hilton's sliding doors in time
to hear *Jose can you see*.

II

Thisness

Thisness

After every poem about mountains, this horst,
      This poem about mountains,
and after every poem in praise of birdsong, this duet
of loggerhead shrikes.
      this poem about birdsong,
After every stormy landscape
in an old gilt frame, this waxing lyrical,
      this waxing
and after each sun-gilded summit, another desperate ascent.
      and waning of the element,
      the black peak-caught clouds
      of winter bluster across the water,
After every riparian song, this creek,
      the thick and thin of that river we followed and crossed,
      wobbling on the spanning log,
and after every serpentine river, this tangle
of watery thoughts, this riffle and babble.
      turning pinched air thick with words, which are water,
After every stuffed and mounted specimen, this bird,
trapped and banded.
      and quick like the woodpecker's knocking
After every dappled scene, meet the elements anew:
ice, light, cloud, and wind, which is breath.
      to answer the world's demands,
And after this poem is read to the wind,
bury the script in talus
to trill from shadows, shrill as a marmot's signal
      that afternoon we watched for goats on hills above the highway,
and brittle as a snake's rattle.
      roads and slopes dry as a snake's jettisoned skin,
After this step, that one, always the same
as the one before the last.

and the soonest star
that pricked the cornflower
as we crossed the ridge
and descended into night on the eastern bank
And before this step, hundreds and thousands
of the same.
—all this accrues as pieces of shale
on desiccated moraines.
And after this poem, every poem about mountains.

~ **Obstruction Point; Hoh River**

Ecosystem

In the house
with no walls,
in the river
with no source
and no mouth,
nothing is
connected
to nothing
and spills over
everything.

Square

Four sides enclose vacancy
and frame a vital blank.
Snow, shock, nix—a field
on the verge of escape.

Schist

The gods speak. I take
dictation. When
I talk they take no
notice, and what
I write I cannot
read. What else did
I expect? What more
could come of lichen's
grip, of stone's
cleaving palms?

First, Failure

I wanted words so dense
that no light could escape,
so powerful their gravity
that sound would be consumed.

I sought a touch of leaves
so soft that I could sleep
in reddened grace. But preying
branches scored my head,

snagged my coat. I ducked,
tripped, blundered. Impeccable
thoughts failed to come to mind.
I wanted the sinister globe

to spin in my right hand,
errant, total, an obsidian
vortex to compel and devour
me—or to stay at a distance

so vast that its expression
would demand unnerving
figures and exotic, shimmering
units. I could not conjure

what I wanted to be. Unfit
for my task I dallied
in eddies, undrowned
by revolving pools. Black as ink

was all my words could be.
Nothing stuck to my Teflon tongue.
Dense, I see, means *stupid*, means *dull*.
I spoke an absolute null.

Failure Revisited

Then I wanted to speak with only
two words, a brute lexicon of nil—
to be austere, as callous

as the cloudless sky, precise
as the switchbacking path
through rubble to the pass,

to navigate by the compass
of a red-tailed hawk's mind.
But I couldn't stop talking.

The jibber-jabber of sparrows
and the whoomp-whoomp-whoomp
of a copper grouse discharged

into precipitate flight by footsteps—
their uncareful speech is not
without rhythm and meaning.

The grouse and the air
that it drums rehearse silence.
The two words? *This* and *that*.

Eclipse

When the hand opens,
when the hand is opened,
when the hand has opened,
when the hand opening
reveals nothing,
nothing happens.

When the mind opens,
when the mind is opened,
when the mind has opened,
when the mind opening
invites the wind's winter,
nothing happens.

And when the heart opens,
when the heart is opened,
when the heart has opened,
when the heart opening
admits red lunar light,
nothing quickens.

A Premise in Kamloops

Ice on the river's surface is not melting
but only becoming itself. The running
water is not melting the frozen layer
but beckoning itself to follow.

Spell for the Museum of the Canadian Rockies

Rundle, Cascade, Sulphur, Norquay
Candle, Rascal, Camphor, Belay
Gamble, Disaster, Nevermore, Spray
Bangle, Faster, Silver, Delay

On the razorback
ridge near the end
of endless winter
no one speaks. Cloaked
cracks croon mutely
to nascent creeks
and warble intricate
summitward routes
that firn and ice,
fissures, rockfall
and time betray.
Lonesome stones
gather themselves
for the long,
unroped descent.

Angle, Crisis, Aster, Dismay
Sulphur, Cascade, Rundle, Norquay

To Gordon Burles

On Tuesday morning
in your bookstore on Caribou Street
you set me straight
about Inglismaldie and the Finger,
Girouard and Assiniboine,
as Jon Whyte, you said,
set Earle Birney straight
once upon a time
in the West of blessed memory.

Now Earle, Jon, you, and I
all know which mountain faces
which exacting mountain.

You poets of Banff—
you climbers and sticklers!
You learned how to breathe
this thin air well. You see
the sedimentary thought
pulsing in the troposphere.

Sunplay on Mountains

after Kenneth Rexroth

The eucalyptus there,
the arbutus here,
and the manzanita
are paper.

The boulder here
and the talus there
are paper too.

And you are paper
on which talus,
boulders, arbutus
and eucalyptus write.

At sunset all is grey
from sand to stratus
save the outlying
snowfield—coral
smouldering like split
and polished manzanita.

In the Spirit World, on a Rock

Late sun sits. Granite
is warm but not hot.
Wind whistles but softly.
This perch is wide enough

and just long enough
for a pause to be not
altogether uncomfortable.
What rests? Pain. A nest

of kingfisher eggs. Gravity
and midnight. But this is not
our world, no. This dusky
world is not ours at all.

High Meadows, September

Oh, we need winter to come
and its chill. The air has been heavy
with summer too long. We want to die,
the larches say, and wake up
stripped, spare, braced for the year.

When you have nothing to give
and nothing has dug in, rooted
itself in earth and ice, the pines
say, then cold will blossom,
no current run, and what
survives begin to die afresh.

Salmon Reconsidered
Goldstream River

When all the fish have died
or escaped upstream
to perish; when the sky
is clotted with squawking,
squabbling gulls; and when
the sated river is dammed
by bloating silver—
then nothing can be said.

Hooked on Mount
Finlayson's low outcrops,
freshets of mist
from the Strait envelop
the exhibition. Then
everything remains
to be uttered.

In Winter's Nick

In the first hours below freezing an acute
clarity, once latent, cuts into sunlight,
keening the day as some birds sing *C*
and woodpeckers hammer *O*. It letters the air
with an alphabet of none, making plain
what bashful maples mutter. It rings, that tune,
that tunnelling strain. Some ignore the cold
that planes the sky, that lightly sings: *you will die*.

Seasonal

Cold nights you craved relief, the insipid sameness
of flawless days and ceaseless summer.

In morning sun you welcomed Arctic
inklings, the ripening chill of fall's decay.

In times of blizzard and snowslide, thoughts
of verdant change assuaged you who knew

long seasons of bright torment. Don't languish
now after passing time or pine for dog days

as merciless as constant winter. Dark will come
and light again, even if only December's

flat, sober glow. All change holds a river's
elegance, its propensity to flood.

For the Millionth Time

The leaden sun
glissaded
into slate
water and rose
weightless from waves,
lifting itself
into crisp,
brilliant, severe
circularity.

Maundy Thursday

... Nicholas' frontal bone
Walled out a clouded world
—Ted Hughes

Sudden bells surprised me
before the calendar
quieted the mystery: Easter,

late, had blown in. Iron clouds
conspired to let fly
a hailstorm, disclose

a teasing rainbow. Pellets
were tokens, raindrops icons.
Ice and arc bloomed as riddles

on the other side of windows.
So I ventured out
to be pummelled by cold

pebbles. The thick bone
above my eyes, the sheer face
of my face, was no fortress

wall but a ruined fence
dividing nothing from nothing,
a plinth propping up ether.

Although the belfry rang
matters of the soul, the sky's
bravura clangour intoned:

in every leaf, lupercalia—
in each sprig, the wolf's howl,
its footfalls in snow.

Invocation

When I met you
I knew nothing
of consequence.
I came from an
unnamed place
and saw only
the lack of light.
You gave me salt,
citrus, an elm,
a crow, and all
this with a glance.
My name became
yours, and ours
the river's rustle
under late snow.

III

Instructions
for Travel

Instructions for Travel

Go seaward, dissident—
to lower land where
the plashing drink
tells you no
and again no. Death
is with you here.
Descend to the river,
novice—let water
solve your dryness. Admit
your solidity as liquid
gushes and roils, sending
up spume as proof
of change. While steelhead
in the current press
on, pursuing stoneflies,
go, friend, to the hill
on which duration
waits. Set foot, pilgrim,
in the marsh where covert
life teems. Go down
to the lowest canyon
to die beneath the piñon
pines. Come back to sea
level and live. Listen,
you must lose yourself.
Let the words you have
always been forgetting
leave you. Touch your tongue
to trees. Dip your eyes
in streams and give
your ears, stranger,
to the wind. Grasp
the pumice in your mind.

Teachers and Pupils

From the air you study the land
as if it were a map—
four-cornered, bounded, uncreased,
and entirely transparent.
But ah, the mountains adazzle
say, *our fickle heights
are infinite. Each field of ice,
each band of metamorphic
rock—a cosmos.*
                        The cap
of perpetual snow on Olympus
is frozen as cannot be glimpsed
from above. Birds' eyes
are impermeable.

But a hand in the snow
feels cold's clench keenly
and its latticed breath.

A Lesson on Mount Rexford

The technique is straightforward: push
both strands through the belay
device's slots into the carabiner.
Lock the gate, fasten a Prusik
cord to the rope: it will jam
if left untended—if you lose
consciousness, say, or simply let
your brake hand slip—and you will
hang safely in suspension. Check each point
of connection. Weight the system,
squat to test it. Unclip the back-up
line. Now the real thing: step back
over the lip, let the harness
hold you, your adherent soles
pressed against the stone. Thirty metres
down you will reach the ledge, retrieve
the rope, go home. If you neglect
to secure the ends, of course,
you may quite effortlessly
lower yourself into free fall.
It is advisable to tie them
together unless your intent
is not to descend but by
intricate and elegant means
to make as if by magic
one substance from another,
to turn the body's water into air.

Late August, Nesakwatch Spires

Flies buzz, and a stifling light bleaches west
faces in this corner of the Cascades
while the breeze holds its breath. Then from below,
an echoing *fuck*. Off the sub-summit
I rappel, dangling in space as I peer
past my feet to sight flat ground. My friend, first
to descend, sits out of view, slightly shocked
in a gravelly hollow, paper wrappers
strewn about after a raid on the first-
aid kit. A tickle from a granite flake—
now we need butterfly bandages
to stop the laughter. I remember
that last week in a nearby range someone
wandered off. A broken leg, maybe, or
a slip into a fissure that the chopper's
eye missed, and a long, last intermission.
True, we're only weekenders pretending
to adventure. True climbers would simply laugh:
while extemporizing prodigies work steep
new routes and masters of the repertoire
play mountains with style, I'm stuck on scales
and basic footwork. I rehearse: this descent,
like our upward path, is easy enough. What
could go wrong? Nothing more than banged-up knees,
sandpapered elbows, scabby knuckles.
Under the outcrop we scan the fleshly damage;
we could reach the hospital by nightfall.
Our third lowers himself blindly down
the rope, takes pictures, tells us to get going:
it's time to eat. I stuff bloody gauze
into the pack as my friend walks it off,
a batter hit by the pitch.

                    Games at heights
should be played without regard for simple
setbacks, and if my next task is to stitch
minor accident and lack of chops
to the sterile page, to render trivial
episode into parable, then I must
have missed the point of this excursion.
I should take it in stride, find no meaning
or cause for alarm in a tibial glimpse.
But megrims rush in: will I risk it all
for a peak or line? Will I watch the fall
when the bombproof handhold moves for the only
time in a thousand years, peels away
from the wall to expose fresh rock, and takes
with it the body that weighted it so
lightly? Will I defend the vanity
of resisting mass and mechanics? What
if? What if? The questions would keep us
safely inside and brooding. Soon the puckered
peek at chance and loss will heal and life,
as they say, will go on until it doesn't.
On this white field, though, nothing closes.
Time's pricks draw blood: that gravity presses
in mind, releases a biting sorrow
that would melt Alpine snow. If this landscape
doesn't get us, it'll be the flu or
the bus when I forget to look both ways.
Shit, shit. The world hates us sublimely
and both desperado and homebody
should hear the creaking door, the ticking clock.
It is too much with us and not enough,
and refuses our stupid love's advances.
Wounds tended, I scutter down the gully
to base camp and mutter to the basin
my stony ultimatum. *Watch out: I
forget nothing and forgive even less.*

Snow Dome

The glacier-shuffle's over. Now we get serious—
time to suffer, to conquer this bitch. *Let's go.*
(First we dither, hydrate, fiddle with crampons,
axes, lights, packs. The arsenal can't rescue

us from ourselves. It's amateur hour on the wall.)
Scared, rimed, we quit before we start—unheroics,
face unsaved. Now here comes some sweaty yahoo,
clueless, shirtless—a jumbo tourist on his way up,

too late to be safe. Grisly sun has softened
snow bridges. Crevasses skulk. Day's end looms.
No rope, no helmet, no way down: he's naught
but sunburn, oily belly, scraggly hair. But the yeti

of unpreparedness won't be stopped.
He ignores advice and gets moving. *So long. Good
luck.* For days and bodies I scoured the papers. No
sign of life was found. No cars were abandoned

at the trailhead. He must therefore have made
it back alive, or he's out there climbing still.
Yes—he needed no ride. He strolled to the base
with impossible strides. Soloists leave

no friends behind. He went over the summit
and ate the cornice, followed glaciers, the Humes, the Hoh,
into far Alpine wastes. Now he hunkers down
in the bergschrund at night, dining on ice-

fall and hoarfrost. He grows heavier, shaggier,
more defiant of gravity and logic. The Fat Man
on Snow Dome is himself a crevasse, a blue
absence into which the normal course falls.

~ **Mount Olympus**

On Reading *Conquistadors of the Useless*, by Lionel Terray

In these blue badlands we wear the Alps
and Patagonia from head to the ground
but never step outside. Our baseball caps
smack of dutiful days; the desky tang
of espresso cups sticks to us like resin
from the knobcone pines on which we scratch
polypropylene minds. Hobos of the living
room, vagrants of the bibliothecary,
circumambulators of condominium
courtyards, dirtbag masters of sixteen-hour
workdays, coffeeshop habitués, ski-
dreamers, route plotters, high-definition
video streamers, we costume with canvas
and flannel, stop shaving and stink.
We have down jackets of every bloody weight.
Supremely synthetic, we're waterproof
in all colours. Sitting, we grip low pile
carpet and kick, the flex of honeycomb-
cored sticks pushing us up ideated
slopes. Couloirs beckon. Ledges call. We stop
our ears with fluoro wax and read whole
internets of nada, snacking on belay
devices, IsoPro fuel, artisanal
cheeses, nylon webbing, magazine mulch.
Expensively shaggy haircuts hide
under toques of all the rainbow's neon shades.
Reflected in the iridescence
of our polarized lenses are dying dragonflies,
their compound eyes all but invisible.

Mountain Failure

To start I'd sprain an ankle
(twist it at a frightening angle).

Then halfway up I'd turn back
and claim I'd lost the track

to hunger, weather, caution, thirst.
Or near the summit I'd lose my grip

and plummet down the steep, shaly scree.
Off the face I'd feel my fingers slip:

I'd accelerate at little g,
flailing like a fledgling parachutist, headfirst,

failed in nerve, deficient in skill.
Or descending I'd untie the rope.

It'd slither through the carabiner and tumble down the slope.
Then on the overhang I'd learn what the mountain will

in the slow millennia about humility,
endurance, erosion—about the constant t.

Mount Rundle

Second Attempt: 18 September

Up at 6:00. Gone by 6:20.
In lieu of coffee, Diet Coke (2 cans) en route. In lieu of food, four
        Pop-Tarts, untoasted (calories: 800).
43 minutes direct to the trailhead. Temperature: 4 degrees.
47 minutes hiking up to the Central Gully.
Snack in the snow (knee-deep): Diet Coke (1 can), energy bar
        (calories: 250).
Temperature: -5. Low light at 8:00. Piss: clear as the sky
        if only the sky were clear.
Fifteen hundred vertical metres to gain the summit.
Fifteen kilometres from door to door.
To measure: watch, map, compass.
To see: headlamp. To balance: carbon-fibre poles. To remember:
        camera.
Above the treeline: gravel on slabs, new snow on gravel, ice on bare
        dolostone. On the way back, past the familiar gully:
        boiling water for mint tea
        and the trudge down eroding switchbacks.

Or in other words,
Blindness, starglister, moonlight, cloudwisp,
two elk bounding downslope, startled by my panting.
Grey light ascending the gully and snow claiming ground.
An interlude with the crest at last in sight,
a gasp of lifeless air,
and the drawn-out apprenticeship
to the oxygenated world.

Avalanche Bulletin

There is a fundamental asymmetry to understanding avalanches.
It is much easier to recognize conditions leading to 100% certainty
of avalanches than it is to recognize that the snow is 100% stable.
　—The ABCs of Avalanche Safety

And the snows come hurrying from the hills
　—Emily Dickinson

The recent storm snow will turn moist
almost immediately when touched
by the sun. Expect loose
avalanches to occur
as soon as the day begins
to warm up. Avoid exposed slopes
when solar radiation is strong,
especially if snow is wet.

Conditions should concern
any backcountry traveller
for the rest of the season!

Stay diligent when assessing
size of slope, consequences
in shallow areas within
the snowpack. Overnight clearing
and temps in the -10
to -15 range mean
incandescent skies
in the morning.

Freezing level to 1800 metres
should maintain the crust,

depending on exposure.
No new avalanches observed.

Intense sun, daytime heating,
high overnight freezing levels
cause slides in steep terrain. Start
trips early. Get out before
things heat up. Watch for clues
—cliffs sloughing—that the pack
is warming. Travel before
the heat of the day. Avoid big
slopes in the afternoon. Have fun
out there. Don't die. Not yet.

At Bozeman International, in Hugo Country

Dick, your people are here at the rotten
bar that stretches only half as long as
the clouds in that sky as big as promised,

half as long as the Bridger Range. Sunset
now, and I've had a pint for us both. My flight
to Seattle, your other country, will depart

in darkness, chase light to the blinking coast.
On the way down the Gallatin, 191,
the shuttle driver claimed the bison

were Ted Turner's, and I wouldn't dream
of disagreement. Buddhist, they paid traffic
no mind. Cowboys, fishermen, drinkers,

Yellowstoners: old and faithful are here
catching the pink behind Belgrade's
water tower, dispatching final photos

before the boarding summons. For some few
there's time to tilt at lotto terminals. I turn
to see a tele lens trained on bearish me:

this poem, Dick, has ruined a perfect
shot. You're nowhere, drowned in the Kicking Horse,
your fat words remembered by some, yes,

but powerless to get us home and dry.
That drive was a miracle, you'd agree.
First clear afternoon all week, bugs galore.

We passed rubbery men in the river
making love to rainbows and, if they got
lucky, maybe cutthroat. For my days in this state

I thank Chet Huntley and God. Lone Mountain
presides over ski run–ruined slopes
in all directions. New roads bring jobs, they say,

and cash. I scrambled to the summit—eleven
thousand feet, which is airless enough
for maritime lungs, and I found no stone

to carry down, not even a spent shell
left by the avalanche crew (a vessel
trailside notices warn not to touch)

or an empty canister of capsaicin
spray, amulet against the dread grizz. All
the signs in the wide world won't save us, all

the sentiment. Were you here drunk on beer
or ice cream (I admire your divided
loyalties), you would hardly recognize

my pain, nor I yours, but maybe common
ground lies in terrain itself, in fishy stream
and the horizon where domains converge.

I'll leave you to one more. They've called all those
with millions of miles, and men and women
in uniform. Thank you for your service.

Contra Naturam

Do not send poems involving birds, wings, feathers or flight.
        —Instructions for submitting poetry to a literary journal

Have we lost all sense of how to behave when we fly?
        —Headline

Turbulence. The airflow's agitation
persists but is not constant.
Mountains may be to blame,
or vertical currents of air, or jet

streams, or strong winds. The seat-
belt sign is illuminated
at the captain's discretion. Reduce speed.
Change altitude. Consult pilot reports

and hope for the best. The men in hats
do what they can up front. In 32F
you wait it out. It's not natural,
flying like this, but your Aeroplan

points multiply like idiomatic
rabbits. Wingless, otherwise marooned,
unfeathered, inept as the kakapo, you
surrender to conditions and providence,

time and design. On the ground it is
the same. Your venerable oxygen-
processing machinery steams
from overuse. Ocular instruments

wear out; perambulation gear
is fated for the Salvation Army.

It's a miracle you're here at all.
Sit back, relax, read the laminated

instructions for not dying. This swell
has lasted for hours, is old as the hills.
Consider the tranquil, unsullied
waxen bag. Ponder cooler creatures

somewhere between the brink of existence
and the threshold of extinction: the snoring
rail, a panda with a quiff, a reckless
cougar with a Kawasaki motorcycle,

the hexapus, the rare dodecapus,
bookish krill. On the ocean floor
phosphorescence turns spelunking fish
into reading lights. Your seat drops

a foot. Animal lessons, like the cockpit
and drinks cart, are just out of reach.
In the extremely unlikely event
that you make it, thank the unassuming

birds, whose behaviour is beyond
reproach. Oh God. O gods! O
cormorants, skimmers, cranes—how
do you weather us, endure our mimicry?

In Midair

Antarctic glacial melt rate triples in Amundsen Sea embayment
—*Headline*

You love no one as much as maps. On interminable
flights, black arcs at the back of the free magazine

all come to point north and west. They lead
past the Brooks Range toward Nome

and nowhere. Each curving, indelible
route veers away, bends bloodshot eyes

to follow, and tows you to lonely Prudhoe Bay
and pipelines. In King Salmon, Alaska, what else

but fish, those who catch them, boats that ferry
from dry to death, docks that give hypothermic

trawlers respite before the next run? Another
skyline. You drift in and out of artful sleep.

No one sits with you but alluring,
frostbitten names that hook you

who should know better than to bite that fly.
Cometh the hour, approacheth the keepers

with menus, headphones, credit card
swipers. You are plied with nuts and soda.

What a world it is that robust Coca-Cola
and Diet Coke cruise together at thirty-five

thousand with their dour companion, Coke
Zero. Crude gushes to the terminus, makes

us rich. Fuck the caribou with their concave
hooves, who'd have done the same to us if

they'd thought of it first, and screw the clean-
up crews that cuddle slick gulls on the coiling

news. Let them eat lichen. Let them wolf
down a sachet of pretzels and enjoy

a glass of Exploration Merlot
or Pinot Gris from Canoe Ridge Vineyard

in oniony Walla Walla. It's a greasy
business, life. What's left to discover

in wine or boats? Not much. As you sip
the black cipher from your plastic demi-cup

and crunch cubes like the *Yermak*, your cavity
grows. *Return of the Secaucus*

7 plays unheard on the tiny screen.
You love no one as much as maps, their bows

and blanks, though Kamloops sage and harbour
brume buoy you up, it's true, and juniper, pitch,

and snowberries aflame in sun. May time
and tide wait for nomads in complete silence.

The dinging means strap in. Come to.
What goes up is revived by rising ground.

Disembark, step into the cancerous
smell of gasoline or whatever fuels

flying machines, and spy the Arctic
emptiness on the low horizon.

Transcontinental

"Puget Sound's killer whales continue decline":
the news this morning, nearly summer's last,

can't possibly be news. Here on the continent's
right side, I'm no more useless to the overgrown

penguins, no less, than I would be at home, not far
from Orcas Island. Horcasitas, Viceroy of Mexico,

was the namesake, books say. But who cares? I hear
that old, cropped *nombre* and every time think

of cold-blooded whales, the harbour seals
they eat, and tottering ferries full of snappers

waiting for their moment. Becoffeed, benumbed,
I recline with the *Globe* and Geoffrey Hill's

Collected. Near Vatnajökull, magma
simmers, cascades. The great eruption looms.

When we drown in ash, when the orcas throw
in the towel—then I'll be impressed. At dinner I met

someone whose friendly neighbour in childhood
was the Ant, Spilotro, Tough Tony. We chatted

mobsters, murders, how gambling in Nevada
isn't what it used to be. Small talk, tall fish

tales. But the other week on the MV
Chelan—the Salish name is said to mean

"deep water" (good fortune for a boat: may
all channels be deep, all bays protected)

—I watched a single white-sided dolphin stake
everything on its arc into light, its splash

and vanishing. I stepped from the *Chelan's* ramp
onto the dock in sleepy Anacortes

with its marine supply store, which I love,
and then back to our uncivil, unkind

domain—the dry thoroughfares, the chatter,
the rush that admit little of underwater

life or the parenthesis of the beaked,
birdlike whale breaking from below. Two deaths

this year, the morning news has it. No calves.
What good is gazing? Twenty-five hundred

miles away, I set out now to play sightseer.
In the Memorial Transept on Quincy

Street, the rows of Union dead, cavalcades
of starched, upright, four-square monikers,

look across the suitably heavy air
to counterparts on the opposite wall

and down at pods of craning tourists while
the wooden door groans and thumps. Come September,

come the new day, the sun will be out, I'm sure,
over Orcas. Meantime the dust in the vault's

humid murk is lit up against stained glass.

Cancer magister

Third week in a new city and again,
scuttled by sleeplessness, I tried to take
the wrong way home. I had to backtrack, reverse
my moves on Franklin to regain the path.
Retreating, making sideways, awkward
progress, I thought *crabwise*, meaning *idiot*.
A neighbourhood dog barked his objection. Some
crabs walk forward and backward: it's true.
Libinia emarginata, which
you may also know, if you too have read
the encyclopedia, as the nine-
spined or portly or common spider crab;
Mictyris platycheles, Down Under;
Raninidae, the frog crabs. *Crabwise* tells
a tale, but not the whole story, in which
respect it's not unlike *doglike, horsey,
bovine, snaky*. Not every ox is as
strong as an ox. Some worms never turn.
The last street but one before my shell
is Pleasant: mornings the balmy statement
is generally true. Come summer solstice
the sun enters the zodiac's fourth sign.
Crabby babies grow up to be homebodies.
They're ruled by the moon, which means, I think,
they waltz ahead and are rebuffed and run
up the shore again. But what do I know?
I was born a bull. This crab-related
disquisition is a stub. You can help
by expanding it, or by releasing
me from curiosity and the need
to remember. Let me make the right turns
on autopilot, fall asleep without
panic. What's wrong? Routine paranoia.

Drought in California. The coming shake.
The shittiness of the world that will last
until the world ends. The magisterial
Dungeness crab, my emblem and anchor,
a little Loch Ness Monster in the remote
New World, its name a small slice of Kent,
vanishes under sand when enough's enough.
In this state I'm banished from our usual lookout,
from which we stare across the Juan de Fuca
Strait at the spit and lighthouse that share
a common name with *Metacarcinus*
magister, as Oregon's state crustacean
is most properly known. The critters can live
two presidential terms. In supermarkets
sit rows of flesh on ice, and sometimes tanks
of rubber-banded pincers kept alive
to remind us of desperation.
The Whole Foods on River Street sells every
comestible known to man. Unnoticed from
escalators and churchlike aisles, the Charles
flows past the store to Boston Harbor. God,
let me off this cushy hook. A bag in each arm,
I stalk home. Speaking strictly, crabs do
not have tentacles. But *tentare* (to try, to feel)
seems the right verb for crabwise crabs and us.

Cycling

Collisions concentrate the mind.
The first time, I went head-
first into the passenger side
as if to split the car in two.
The Lexus spurned my bike:
I made the intersection my own
little Kitty Hawk, piloting myself
in straight-line flight, a last-ditch
twist of the neck no good.
I crunched. I snapped. A thick part
of my skull smacked the black panel.
I bounced onto the road and lay
in the dark, on my back, in the way,
convinced of physics. The next time,
decked out like a racer, I skidded
across the street. Synthetic fibres
melted in advance of my skin.
Later I scrubbed Lycra
out of my hip until the clean
wound shone like a new coin.
And when a brawny trainee nurse
coarse-clothed gravel out of my shins
and let raw flesh catch its wayward breath,
neither art nor philosophy
offered consolation. Between takeoff
and landing, as gravity clears
its throat, you await metamorphosis.
Silent, solo, you hope to return
to routine. This poem is for my mother,
who worries, and the drivers, God bless,
whom I remember each night when I undress.

The Earthquake

—your first, you said,
terrified you. Unused
to shaking, not trained by years
of schoolroom drills
to wedge yourself against
the incredulous door jamb
or under heavy furniture,
you faced away from windows,
turned your back to disorder,
your delicate neck.

I imagine you then,
readied for disaster, schism
and liquefaction, not yet
having learned a coastal
nonchalance or mastered
the camber and senseless sway
of unstable places, cities
that demand sea-legs
and a strong crawl.

Once during a mild but lasting
tremor, I peered through the office
door, baring my gullet
to glass. A glaucous-winged
gull, disturbed from its dumpster,
rounded the scattered trash, landed,
resumed its affairs. The rest of us,
bird-brained, prattled
like pigeons before nestling
into chairs, screens, pages.

Rough calculation and a taste
for likely stories suggest
a congruence: it was this upheaval
that startled you. Now unbalanced
by more than seismic waves and gods'
displeasure, I study what inland
people know, what compensatory
sense you gained long ago
when you left the ocean behind.

On Corporeal Existence

Ignore the minor earthquakes
that throw bodies off balance,
exposing faults and fractures.
Pretend abrasion only gnaws
at far-off crags and dunes.
Forget that knees buckle and fold
as gracefully as tectonic plates
collide and crumple. That mildew
creeps in, powers recede. That skin
capitulates to acuate stone,
drawing back to proffer the bone.
Stricken, dumbstruck, pale
as a page, you see clearly:
the parts are gimcrack,
the workmanship slapdash,
although the contraption still stands,
the ramshackle whole
marginally greater than the sum.
That trembling was just a truck
rattling by. An eastbound freight
train. Yes, a low-flying jet. Straighten
the pictures. Reshelve the books,
the persistent dishes. Put the Big One
out of mind and suture your wounds.
Or cherish them. Draw fingers
over a grizzling face; trace wraithlike
scars before daybreak. Turn warmth
into anaesthetic. Christen
the involuntary flicker of muscle
in spasm and the crooked collarbone
beautiful, taking imperfection
as evidence of survival. Discover
art in fickle skin's treason. Claim cataracts

and cicatrice as translucent gifts.
Your aching jaw holds its shape.
Your raw, rasping throat spins
wheeze into words. Wear weakness
as a talisman against perfection
and our meddling, middling intellect.
Praise these lapsing, third-rate
bodies. You don't have long.

IV

Metamorphoses

Metamorphoses

Quick syluer hath dyuerse tymes fallen out of the cloudes
—*Fulke,* A Goodly Gallerye

The de Havilland Otter bound for Lake Union
leaves the harbour with ten passengers aboard.

The West Antarctic ice sheet, the *Times* reports,
is melting unstoppably. Here come the seas!

Hurricane Ridge, a mile high, is gone, effaced
by fog. Chum and cod in their element hide

from sight. The Pacific halibut, a righteye flounder,
will grow taller than any man. Larvae start

life with an eye on each side. Then the left orb
migrates to the right plane. Good god, nature

is strange. *Hippoglossus* means horse tongue. Homer,
Alaska, is the Halibut Capital of the Universe.

In the Bering Sea bucking fish whinny and see
half of everything exceptionally well. The poet

said the ocean's another country. Whoso longs
to be skate or bird, basalt or tuff, looks skew-whiff

too. Nearly fallen out of the clouds, the playful weasel
splashes onto the blue lid of the underworld.

The Beasts

My people are muskoxen, meerkats, wild
dogs and snow leopards and geese of all kinds,
biting insects, unnamed specimens unknown
to science, the capitalist kittens
who shill, adders, asses, manatees, and goats
leaping into spring on everlooping
videos, the dugong, the narwhal, ostrich,
vireo, emu, moa departed
but not forgotten, killers wingèd, land-
bound, amphibious, and the bovine,
ursine, ovine entities that wield their bulk
upon us, oblige us to stare
at their odd heft. The beasts, the beasts!
Vegetarians and bloody butchers!

In the beginning the world was not formless
but form alone, shape not congealed
into static dominions. Earth ran
quickly as steep rivers sublimated
into volcanic mist. The fuse burned fast
and the phoenix globe was born over
and hotly again. Creatures in multitudes
are proof of fire. I sing the fish that walk
on land. I yelp the mass not yet ready
to be fired into final physique—fixed
till it shatters and shards of azure clay
dissolve and flare at once. I have read it
in salt flats, watched it on hotel TV
late in snowy foothills of the Rocky
Mountains, seen it from the window
seat of the Boeing 767
circling to genesis. Pronghorns
gallivant. Yellowstone wolves swim

frozen lakes. When the sun evaporates,
it is forty below. My cousins persist,
swaddled in peerless nip, beacons
aflame, disclosing the sane path through what some
call wilderness. Pelts are scarred
or striped or spotted with ash. The pages
of *National Geographic* scald
prurient digits. In the small hours, groomers
drive snowcats, Prinoth Beasts, over ski hills,
leaving meringues and wakes of corduroy.

New England Aquarium

Nature / Can only love herself.
      —W.H. Auden, "Oxford"

I

Bears of Nazareth and Juneau, conifers
of Damascus and Leechtown, fishes of Port-
au-Prince and Narragansett, wolves of night
and daybreak—all are filled from rump to ruff,
from tooth to lynx's tuft, root to needle, with
wasps' buzz, pine sap, shade of the Cascades frog's
dorsal spots, the spark of heatless artificial
suns in flickering jellies through which current
runs. Creatures, come: smash cymbal and tympanum,
honk kazoos, strike out these words, play animate
songs. Love, Nature can only sing herself.

II

Come, call on ribboned life behind crystal.
The brume of days upon days has lifted.
Drifting starfish break from black water as
suddenly as stars spring from indigo
skies. We will write new elegies as new years
arrive. Let us chatter then about our
centuries' and cities' failings; let us
discourse later of the worsening chop.
Harpooned and drowned, those of us sprung from flame
yet cling to the view that only flame will
torch us. Where we have been is where we will
burn; where we became coal, we will inhale.

III

Coastal giant salamanders retain
their gills. Pain noses toward us. A straining
hollow insists: *You are unloved by time
and nature unsatisfied.* Two wolves ring
the buzzer; a sponge drinks our tea. Although
they are legion, the signs are illegible.
Our weirs and nets catch only tiring fish,
a puzzle of sparrows, a scare of grackles,
a bundle of kites, a kettle of crows,
and not the light, the magnetic north,
we need and know we need in our dire south.
Love, Nature can only save herself.

IV

Lit jellyfish float in a dark glass tristesse.
Timed jets flush anemones next door with
oxygen. Past the crush roosts the ample
gift shop ruled by stuffed emperors; harbour
seals wait for dental inspection; and sunglare
descends, my beloved, the caving steps
of the Aquarium stop on the T.

The subway in Boston is known locally as "the T."

Photosynthesis

Fat chloroplasts gulp,
inhale rich lustre, exhale sugar.
Virescent, aspiring

cytovoices salute
spring with honeyed tones,
the dulcet timbre

of doubling, redoubling,
inspiring plastic confections.
In the blaring,

glinting carnival
of foliage, transactions
transpire unseen.

Thylakoid, chloros,
organelle, tarantella:
leafy spells are cast.

Lavender douses
skies. Cherry and plum (tint, brush)
daub the infant air.

From the bog's moss
a glacial thought unfolds:
Arctic starflower.

Horses off the Kitsap Shore

Summon the white horse: this river is a bear.
Let the distant sight of the swimming mare's
dark legs lead you into water pearly with silt.

Rope the roan colt breaking the foamy blue to pull
you downstream to the mouth. Cataracts fall
from source to song. Go past combers into

the rough. Coursing toward islands in the strait,
the sorrel, now a salmon, races in salt
current. Smoking tidewater surges

against the craggy peninsula's fingers.
The Kitsap coast jerks and kicks, rears
and roars, wrings logs and flotsam from the stew.

A black bear stands to sniff and boom:
the torrent pours, plunging from pinnacles
into sea. The chestnut in the waves, rogue foal,

passes through swims full of springers, shoals
of chinook, mackerel. Palomino, skewbald,
Appaloosa splash. The strait is elk, kelp,

mussels, cedars. Follow the grey horse paddling
Puget Sound, that pulsing channel of wolves
and sockeye, but peek at the open clam,

the liquid land that you and horses soon
must tread again—that the piney Dewatto
and Tahuya carve, over which the gloom

of rivers' names hangs like advection fog.

Hot Spell in Wet Country

Clallam County, Jefferson, and Kitsap,
once named *Slaughter*, are golden, jocund
daffodils on the National Drought
Mitigation Center's digital map.

From Lincoln, Nebraska, the chart's dusty
throat croaks our verdict: "Abnormally dry."
Yellow means things are just heating up.
California's crimson, an emergency

red. Updates scroll on screens; dull reports
trickle into earshot, flutter past the mind.
Shasta Lake: lowest capacity since
'77. The stubborn Klamath purports

to run, but salmon see unfavourable chances.
Pioneering critters roam uncovered lands,
claiming born-again virgin territory. O
brave new, et cetera. We've herded thousands

of years of data. Tree rings regret to inform us
that years, decades, whole centuries were dry.
Nothing's new, but no one remembers
the 1580s. *In a drought, the thirsty creatures cry,*

And gape upon the gather'd clouds for rain.
Now sober honeybees drop like enervated flies.
The withering West is a teetotal state.
Once evergreen, we put the word to the test.

What does malign heat augur beyond flame?
(Nature's tone-deaf. We just had record rain.)

Beneath the desert eye, we wait for newfound
fever to flood us. High in desiccating

ranges, everything burns away like sulphur
but silence. When fetid water leaves lakes,
what remains is bleached, intricate,
beautifully reticulated earth,

hard as concrete, dark as glass, pulled taut
—a net strained by suffocating trout.

Spell for the Elwha River

Dam removal began on the Elwha River in mid-September 2011.
Today, Elwha Dam is gone, over fifty percent of Glines Canyon Dam
has been removed, the Lake Mills and Lake Aldwell reservoirs have
drained, and the Elwha River flows freely from its headwaters in the
Olympic Mountains to the Strait of Juan de Fuca for the first time in
100 years.
            —US National Park Service

Sol Duc, Quillayute, come down
fast from the forest, cold to the sea.
Elwha, Elwha, run again,
and sprint, Dungeness, to the spit.

You made a break for it, O misguided,
misdirected river. You burbled
misereres, thinking that you'd prevail.
But we will misremember you, once-
stoppered, once-static bourn, who against
the odds outlasted the century
and us. Have mercy—we only wanted
arms around you. Where glaciers rest in umber,
liquid thoughts form as tight-lipped moraines
keep the peace. Your names are frozen water.
What was taken apart can be rebuilt,
and what we loved we set our hearts on still.

Quinault, Quilcene, Calawah,
give us the slip, slide pell-mell
from the greenwood, stinging to the tide.
And Elwha, Elwha, gallop again.

In Praise of the Mountain Pine Beetle

Dendroctonus ponderosae
Length: about half a centimetre

Decimator, annihilator, ugly fucker,
you stained the Cariboo pines,
making everything kind of blue
and empty. Improviser, virtuoso,
exterior decorator, you rendered
montane monochrome a museum
piece. Propagator, vacationer,
unmarked parcel, part of the furniture,
you love this weather we're having.
You took on the landscape and won.

Pastoral

Tigers at the Oregon Zoo,
asleep in the sultry shade
of the concrete shelter
at the far end of their compound,
tails to the gallery,
listen in their dreaming
to woolgathering polar
bears in the aquarium
half a mile away. Redcedars
and western white pines
span the manicured distance.
Needles and cones
growl and roar, crackling
like telegraph wires.

Auspex Maximus

One who observed the flight of birds, to take omens thence for the guidance of affairs; hence, a director, protector; and esp. the person who superintended marriage ceremonies.
—Oxford English Dictionary

Observer of birds,
come out from the blind:
tell me the names
of your secrets espied.
Abandon your specs,
watcher of skies,
to sing me the ichor
you heard in the cries
of ptarmigan, lark,
kingfisher, crane. Hoist
your scope and guide:
set out in the rain
to chirrup my future
and let the feathered
augury fly.

Sightings

One tern, swift.
Two mallards adrift.
Three hummingbirds hovering.
Four charcoal-winged gulls sorting through junk.
Five untimely sparrows whispering secrets.
Six three-legged paddlebirds nibbling on Greek salads.
Seven yellow-bellied sapsuckers on African safari.
Eight blueberry-tasselled wood-borers navigating odd waterways.
Nine giant scatterbrained witches' finches booking tickets for spring holidays.
Ten mosquito-billed elephant's blood-suckers working their way through
     the dictionary.

Several Birds

How quickly it changed from ash to asp,
that grey goshawk in a gunmetal tree.

How suddenly it turned from stare to snake,
slithering out of the sky.

How abruptly sloop became trap,
snaring a hapless rabbit in half a snap.

But the parrotdox and other fabulous birds—
—the crowned hooplah, the lesser trombone—

dwell in the air, hungry and distracted,
or roost innumerably in bare trees,

pummelled by wind, speared by winter's eye.
They long to be pythons and wolf eels, who swerve

and glide, the birds surmise, with design.
Fanciful fowls wind in flight as aimless rivers

twine through canyons, their changes
as slow as the deepening of limestone walls.

The mildewed thought fidgets in its nest.
The dismal egret regrets everything.

Guillemots et guillemets

The name of several species of sea birds ... esp. Uria or Alca troile,
the Common or Foolish Guillemot, and Uria grylle, *the Black
Guillemot.*
  —Oxford English Dictionary

*Guillemet means Little Willy, in honor of the sixteenth-century
French typecutter Guillaume [William] Le Bé, who may have
invented them. Also called* chevrons, duck feet, *and* angle quotes.
  —*Robert Bringhurst,* The Elements of Typographic Style

Black-breasted auk, *Cepphus,* called William
by friends (Bill by forward acquaintances), quails
at the coming squall, which gathers then wastes
away over the grey wastes: a false alarm.

Calm: and the bird, dumb again, calls silence
from the sea to shelter in his draft.
William the Conqueror, William Rufus,
William of Orange, and the Sailor King,

William IV: dark fowl, historian,
hears in the roll doomsday, internecine
struggle, Whiggery, illegitimate
issue. He falls from the colourless weight

of his stolen, skimmed encyclopedia.
Pale alcid, poor misnamed bird, in search
of signs and clues! Spotted, caught red-footed,
he flees and, scanning distance, spies, tilting

in wind, *V, V, V, V.* Four crotchets, crows
beat slow time. He veers away from the black
marks enclosing nothing. Foolish Guillaume,
would that you could hear the chasing quiet.

Auks Redux

Cepphus on zephyr: still
weather, last long measure
of summer's strain, gives
way to breeze, and lone bird
leaves nest for breath, turns
gasp to berth. Puffin, murre,
dovekie, razorbill skid
across the buffeted
sky, the submerged range
of unclimbed spires,
the lapis tundra. They come
out of spin, up for air,
strike an interval—
minor third, imperfect
consonance—and pitch
onto liquid ice, white
horses chafing at wind.
As when the last auks died
at Eldey, third June,
1844—
a briskly pleasant day.

Migration to the Antipodes

Yes, sheepish Mr. Alenvers rises
at dusk to pour himself two fingers
of breakfast. He winters north of sixty-

seven, keeping eyes on the cold circle's
upward drift. In summer he seeks sticky
eastern cities, sells saunas by the sea.

Pale as the sand, he hawks cashmere and lambs-
wool. As the day begins he coughs up his
dinner—then leaves his nest and skin behind

to snake tail-first to the office, where
he undoes tomorrow's tasks. His *moules*
snap shut in stock; his *frites* burrow into

desert ground. An austral man, he walks
on his head and sleeps face down. His daughters
in their fading years forget familiar

words. At noon he's curled up in the rip's
embrace. Beyond's the soggy, unformed land.
The callow father is child of the strand.

Biography

You were born on a passenger plane
at thirty thousand feet.
You were tied in bowline knots
and left out in the rainless heat

of a Wyoming summer. Tumbleweeds
rolled you into next week
while vultures circled and cowpokes cried.
You slept in the bassinet of a raven's beak.

Your parents were passenger pigeons
but you alone dimmed the blue.
Your brother was a skyscraper
who watched you as you flew

north by nose. When your sixteenth birthday
came you danced with skinks and snails.
Your cake was the temperate rainforest floor.
Your twenties were tough as nails.

Then marriage, houses, children, divorce,
career, betrayal, espionage, pets.
Parturiency, decrepitude, a late renaissance.
The Sorbonne, the Louvre, the Met, the Mets.

When you quit the room, everyone took notice
and imitated your inimical pose.
Your letters were minefields in jewellery boxes:
you wrote a poet's prose.

The Emperor of Ice

Cream is a luxury he cannot afford.
He refuses niceties, speaks only
like water from crusted creeks.
His mouth is clean. A glass of milk
from time to time, but never cream.

He keeps in fighting trim. His belly
is no belly; his torso draws
concupiscent glances. Middle-aged,
he weighs what he hefted in high school,
where he learned the calculus

of crystals. Bid the numb sovereign
chill your temper. This morning's three
cups of coffee, piquant and pungent,
did not thaw him. He looks out coolly
on his empire of shards and seracs.

His crown would drip into his eyes
if he stepped inside to warm his hands.
Indoors does not exist: his palace is snow.
He wears a polar bear on his back. Its head
roosts on his shoulder, its eyes searing the air.

The sultan of ice is king of the beasts.
What burdens does he stomach, benevolent
ruler of the emptiness he surveys?
(There is little ruling to be done
in winter's short, dark days.)

He waits, on top of the world,
pure north, not saintly, claws out,
the last defence against summer's invaders.

From the floes, of no fixed address,
he sends drifting dispatches of cold,

frozen letters dreaming salvation,
asking for tidings from southern realms.
They sing the caribou's heart and slip
away as a harp seal swims under
the hoary film in search of open water.

Grizzly

My two friends are made of snow. The first
stays at home. The second calls no place
her own and roams, breaking trails, tracking

elk. My static pal, curator of No,
utters silence and sets the thermostat
low. Huskies circle the chalet,

barking on his behalf. He keeps a tight,
quiet ship. He quarantines summer.
There's a line past which he will not go.

Towering to see his gelid face, I sniff
the gale, wave, and roar. Sparrows fly
from his arms to my furry nest, yielding bleak

boreal flakes. He stands guard over winter.
My wandering friend is careless, though:
frosty to weather, she leaves herself behind

in temperate terrain. Her coal eyes swim
in hollows. Deliquescent, disappearing,
she trades stasis for tonic reverie, rivering out.

Well, I have my den and my districts too.
I lumber, engaging myself in stands of larch.
(*Engage* meaning "to entangle. ... Obs. or arch.")

He's a sierra; she's a melting cornice.
Alone I scramble over boulders, marking routes.
My nose is my shepherd: I devour smells

and hear the scent of rimy wind. Soon I'll spy
the greatest blue heron, who winters in
the tropics, peregrine, while the snow man

is ensconced in his demesne. I've moseyed
at altitude, seen that revelling gods
hold masques on spires. Breezy Terpsichore

presides over peaks and pikas. I dance to hug
my hibernal companions, the horrible jig
pleasing my circumspect crony. For my

peripatetic I bolero unseen.
Large and ferocious, I perform a twisting
pas de trois with forever and for now.

The Bear and the Wind

I walk like a bear—
I have a bear's gait—
but the gate to the bear's mind is closed.

I smell like a bear—
I have a bear's nose—
but what the bear's paw knows eludes me.

I think like a bear—
I mind what the bear sees—
but the bear's sweep is beyond me.

Oh to sleep the torpid sleep of the dead—
this my hope when my nightmare head
sinks to the soft slab of our bed.

My caved mind races as the wind rushes—
my thoughts are pink-footed shearwaters—
but dark to me is the source of the gale.

As I tread the bridge from vigil
to the far sands' auroral grey,
battering blasts heave up from the beach.

My tattered kite is whipped.
It shudders and crashes.
Pelagic birds waver offshore.

That bear now plodding toward me
does not struggle for words
as cold as the north.

If I could trundle like a bear—
if I could smell like a bear—
if I could think like a bear—

if I could tell the time of the great trees—
if I could open the barred gates—
if I could gather force—

if I could scamper into the bear's mouth
and return—what would be lost?
Would I find you?

Acknowledgements

My poems about nothing did not appear out of thin air. Adam Gopnik's *Winter: Five Windows on the Season* and Robert William Sandford's *Cold Matters: The State and Fate of Canada's Fresh Water* were useful as I wrote about winter. "Whiteout in May": "The Wolf of Winter" and "We Must Be Slow" are titles of poems by Kenneth Patchen; one follows the other in the *Selected Poems* of 1957. My "jibber-jabber of sparrows" in "Failure Revisited" resembles rather closely the "gibber of gulls" in Robert Bringhurst's "Parable of the Indestructible," part of a sequence called *Tzuhalem's Mountain*. I let the similarity stand as a nod of appreciation. "Avalanche Bulletin" was fashioned from reports issued by Parks Canada for Banff, Yoho, and Kootenay National Parks. "Contra Naturam" includes material adapted from *enRoute*, the Air Canada magazine.

Versions of some of the poems in this book were first published in the following journals: *Canadian Literature, Cirque, The Goose, Grain, The Nashwaak Review, The New Quarterly, Prairie Fire, Prism International,* and *White Wall Review*. I thank the editors concerned for their trust in my writing. "The Same Mountain Twice" was published online by *The Walrus* and was included (as "Rainier Twice in a Day") in *Refugium: Poems for the Pacific*, edited by Yvonne Blomer. The poems that appeared in a chapbook published by the Alfred Gustav Press—*Five Sudden Goats:*

Rocky Mountain Poems—benefited from the careful eye of David Zieroth. I am thankful too for the conscientious reading by the anonymous reviewers for the University of Alberta Press, whose helpful suggestions led to a much-improved book.

I am particularly grateful to Peter Midgley and everyone at the University of Alberta Press, and to Alice Major—a most patient editor, always on the qui vive for the right word and the right voice.

And special thanks to Paul Barclay and Jesse Jackson, who have heard it all before.

Other Titles from The University of Alberta Press

Welcome to the Anthropocene
ALICE MAJOR

Poetry, science, ecological calamity, and human-driven climate change. Where do we fit in the universe?

Robert Kroetsch Series

as if
E.D. BLODGETT

Visceral musings from Governor General's Award-winning poet explore the intertwining connection between the human and the natural worlds.

Robert Kroetsch Series

Demeter Goes Skydiving
SUSAN McCASLIN

Award-winning poet exercises the profound mother-daughter trauma forged in the Demeter-Persephone myth with unapologetic modernity.

A volume in the (cuRRents) Series

More information at www.uap.ualberta.ca